The Drum

Written by Michael Lacey Freeman

Illustrated by Bethany Lacey-Freeman & Craig Bulloch

THE DRUM

**Written and illustrated by
Humans for Humans**

Independently Published by:
Michael Lacey Freeman, Italy & UK
Email: michaellaceyfreeman@gmail.com
Website: www.michaellaceyfreeman.com
© All rights reserved.

Published 2024
ISBN: 978-1-7394459-3-5

No part of this book may be reproduced, or stored in a retrieval system, or transmitted in any form or by any means, electronic, mechanical, photocopying, recording, or otherwise, without express written permission of the publisher.

The Drum

Michael Lacey Freeman

Illustrated by Bethany Lacey-Freeman & Craig Bulloch

*I envy the shadow,
of the bottle
in the hall.
It won't break.
It won't fall.
It just stands there so tall.*

Contents

Page

6			Main Characters
8	Chapter:	1	The Sound of Music
14	Chapter:	2	Bus Stop Hero
22	Chapter:	3	The Open Door
27	Chapter:	4	My Drum, My Friend
30	Chapter:	5	Asking
34	Chapter:	6	Not Just Any Sun
39	Chapter:	7	Chimaobi
43	Chapter:	8	A Familiar Face
50	Chapter:	9	A Little Research
54	Chapter:	10	The Midnight Sky
60			The Origin of the Planet Drum
62			About the Illustrators
64			About the Author
66			Lyrics for 'I'm Afraid'
68			Exercises – Test Your Knowledge
85			Stories by Michael Lacey Freeman

Chapter 1:

The Sound of Music

Hi everyone! Are you sitting comfortably? Are you ready for my story?
My name's Nathan. I'm 17 years old and I live in a small town near London. I like living near London because I can go to all the best rock concerts. I love music. I don't care if it's Pop or Rock or Classical or Rap. I like music because I like sounds. There are certain sounds that I like a lot.

I love the sound of the drums. I like to drum on my desk at school, but I can't do it too much because the teacher stops me. I drum on anything, on my legs when I'm sitting down, on the dining table at home, on the walls of my bedroom. Dad says that one day he'll buy me a set of real drums, but I think he's worried about the noise I will make.

I like other sounds too.
The sound a can of coke makes when I open it.
The sound a pen makes on a piece of paper when you are writing.
The sound the toaster makes in the morning when my breakfast is ready.
And the sound of Netflix when I turn on the TV.

'Ba Boom!!!'

I love the sounds of nature too. I like listening to the sound the rain makes against my bedroom window. And the trees moving in the wind.
I listen to the birds singing while I'm on my way to school. When I hear the birds, it feels like I'm part of nature. I feel like I belong to something much bigger than me.

But the sound of music is the sound I love the most. I often listen to the music of my favourite band, 'Crispy Street.' Crispy Street aren't famous or anything like that. They're a local band. They have two albums and I have both of them. I'm their greatest fan. Owen Banks is the drummer of Crispy Street, and he is so good. No one can play the drums better than him.

Every night I listen to music before bed, and I fall asleep very quickly. I need music to fall asleep. I think it's because my mum sang to me when I was little. She always sang the same song to me every night and I closed my eyes and fell asleep to her sweet voice.

I can't hear mum's voice anymore. Mum died when I was very little and now it's just dad and me, two men living alone. I can't sing my mum's song. I don't want to sing it and I don't want to remember it. It will make me too sad. I will cry if I hear it. It's a song from her country, Nigeria. Mum moved to the UK when she was young. Her name was Ngozi.

The music stopped for a long time when my mum died. I have a memory of her that will never go away. Every morning, she woke me up by opening the bedroom curtains. She opened them very gently.
The light of the sun entered the room and then she came to my bed and said to me softly,
'Time to get up, Nathan. *Kulie N'ura.*'
Kulie N'ura means 'wake up' in the language of my mother. Sometimes I wake up to that gentle voice, even now.
'Kulie N'ura'.
This is because when I'm worried and unhappy, mum is in my dreams. How can I explain it? It's like this. When you

are under the water you cannot hear anything. Dreaming is like being under the water. Mum speaks to me in that silent space of my dreams and tells me that everything will be okay.

I know that the voice isn't really there, but it is inside me. It is a part of me. It's a part of me that I am also afraid of, because I miss mum and thinking about all this makes me so sad.

Well, let me get back to the story I have to tell you.

It begins on a very normal Friday evening. I'm on my bed listening to Crispy Street. When I listen to music, normally I can't hear anything else – just the music. But on this particular Friday I do hear something.

'Thud, Bang, Crash!!!'

I look around to see where the noise is coming from. It's raining hard. The rain is beating on my window trying to get in. And the wind is playing its song too.
'It's a storm!' I say to myself. 'But what was that noise?'

I want to find out. And that is why at about 11 pm on a Friday night I put on my coat and some shoes, go into the kitchen, and open the back door to the garden.
I have my mobile phone with me, and I use it as a torch. It helps me to look around the garden. It's difficult to see very much with all the rain but to my left, near the garden shed, I see something. I go closer to the shed so that I can look better. Is it a cup? No, it's too big. A bucket? No, it's too small. I put the torch on my phone a little closer and then I can see a little bit more. Then I look up.

'Where did it come from?' I ask myself. The sky? I can't answer this question. There is no time to answer it anyway. I'm getting very wet and so I bring this thing inside my house.
After taking off my coat, I look at it. It's still very dirty and wet and so I start to clean it. 'It looks like a pot of some kind,' I think.
It has a hole in it, no! Two holes. But it's not broken. The holes are meant to be there.
'It's a gift from the sky!' I smile to myself at this thought, and then start to tap on it for a little while to see what it's made of.

Tap, Tap, Tap!!!

It makes a beautiful sound. I like it and immediately decide to add it to the list of sounds that I like the most. But then I hear another sound, in the distance. It's far far away. It sounds like a door that is opening.

'Creak!!!'

'What was that?' I say to myself.
The sound is very far away. 'It's the bad weather,' I say. 'I'll look at my gift from the sky a little bit better tomorrow.'
Before going back to bed, I look at my phone to check the time.
How is it possible? I was only in the garden for about five minutes!!!

But four hours have passed.

'It's 3am!'

'I'm tired,' I think. 'I got the time wrong when I went out. It was probably much later.'
But I can't really think about time at this moment. The storm has passed. I need to get some sleep. I put the pot in my wardrobe, and start listening to Crispy Street.

Chapter 2:

Bus Stop Hero

'Kulie N'ura.'

I hear mum's sweet voice in my head the next day, and as always it wakes me up.

Dad is angry with me for getting up late. At first, he's so angry that he doesn't notice the pot I have in my hands from last night. I want to take it to the shed and put it in there, but dad is in the kitchen and he's not happy.
'Your lunch will be cold now,' he says. 'You still have to eat it. I made something special. I made some Abacha.'
Now I know that dad is sad. He's always sad when he makes Abacha. It's a fish dish that mum made. It comes from Nigeria, and it's delicious.
'I'm sorry, dad,' I say. 'I like it cold too, so I'll eat it all, I promise.'

Dad smiles. He isn't angry really. He knows that things aren't easy for me without mum. Things aren't easy for both of us.

I start to walk towards the back door. But too late! Dad has noticed that I have something in my hand.
'What's that?' he asks.
'Nothing special,' I say, and dad seems happy with that answer.
'Nothing special' I say, and I believe it too. How wrong I am! But I have no idea at that moment as I go into the garden that what I have in my hands is more than special. It's super-super special.

I go into the shed, put the pot inside, and then return to the kitchen to eat my cold, but delicious lunch.

Abacha!

All the time during lunch I think about the pot. I remember drumming on it, and the special sound it made. I really want to hear that sound again.
I'm excited but I'm not sure about that other sound. That creak sound, like a door opening. What was that? I decide to leave the pot in the shed over the weekend. I just want a weekend without mystery and complication.

It's a great weekend. After lunch I go skateboarding in the park with my friends, Jack and Anne. Jack is waiting for me when I arrive. He has dark hair and green eyes. Some of the other kids at school call him, 'Irish' because his mum is from Dublin in Ireland. He's quite tall and that's why he's so good at basketball.

Anne arrives just a few minutes later. I can see her in the distance as I stand there with Jack. You can't miss her long red hair as it moves in the wind. We find a nice place to do some skateboarding and other friends come along and we chat with them too. I enjoy myself so much that I forget about the mysterious pot.

After skateboarding we go shopping together, not to buy anything really but just to look at things we like.

On Sunday, we spend the morning at the gym, but we don't do very much. Most of the time we talk about things like Crispy Street, and about other kids at our school.
'That new boy at school is cool,' says Jack.

'Who? Mason Adderley?' I ask.
'Yeah,' says Jack.
'He comes from Manchester,' says Anne. 'I've been there. I love it!'
Anne knows so much. She travels much more than Jack and I and she's so clever.
We speak about Mason, but I don't really want to speak about the new boy at school. I want to speak about a new girl at school. Her name is Emma and she's really nice. I like her very much and I want to find an excuse to talk to her. But I don't want to tell Jack or Anne. Not yet. First, I have to get to know her myself a little bit.

After gym I do my homework and then I go to sleep very quickly while listening to Crispy Street. I don't think about the pot, the gift from the sky. I'm too tired.

On Monday morning I make my breakfast before going to school and as I go towards the fridge I look to my left and see the shed from the window.
'The Pot,' I say to myself. I remember the mysterious object again, and I decide to look at it after school.
'Was it all a dream. Did I imagine it?' I ask myself. 'Is it still there?'

As soon as the school day ends, I run back home. I can't wait to go into the garden and see the mysterious object again.
I open the door of the shed, and there it is. It's still a bit dirty and so I take it out and start to clean it a little bit more. While I'm cleaning it, I notice that there's a picture on it. It's a picture of the sun.
'I'm sure that this picture wasn't there before,' I say to myself. 'Where did it come from?'

I put my hands on the pot and start to drum again. I remember the sound I liked so much that night in my bedroom. It does sound like a drum. It is a drum. I'm sure of it now. And I love the sound it makes. I tap more quickly with both hands to make some music.

And I start to lose myself in the music I'm making.

But then, suddenly, I hear that sound again.
The sound of the door.

'Creak!!!'

It's louder this time. And the door feels a little nearer than the last time. I stop drumming.
My head feels strange, like I'm tired. But I'm not tired really. I close my eyes, then open them.
And when I look ahead of me, I cannot believe what I see in front of my eyes.
I'm still in the shed. I know somehow that I'm still sitting there. But my eyes can see something else. Not normal

things that you see in a shed. Instead of these things, in front of me I can see the street outside my school.
It was like I was watching a little movie.
'How is this possible?' I think. 'How can I see these things inside my shed?' This isn't VR. I have no headphones on. I'm in my garden shed, but I'm also somewhere else. I'm looking at the front entrance of my school.

Then the scene changes.

Now, I can see the bus stop just in front of my school. And I can see a girl. I recognise her!
It's Emma. She's the new girl at my school, the girl I like. The girl I don't want to tell Jack or Anne about.
There are two other girls near Emma, who are also wearing the uniform of my school. They're shouting at her and pushing her. Suddenly I see Emma fall to the ground. Who are these girls? One of them looks like Amy. Is the other one Chloe?
'What's happening to me?' I say to myself.
I close my eyes again. And then when I open them, I can't see the bus stop anymore. I can only see the inside of my shed again.
Everything is back to normal. Once again there are only the normal things you see in a shed. 'What was that?' I ask myself. 'I'm tired, more tired than I thought. What's the time? I should sleep.'
I look at my mobile phone and once again my eyes tell me something that doesn't make sense. It's seven in the morning. Tuesday morning!
'What happened to the nighttime?' I ask myself. I didn't have time to answer this question. At that moment there is only one thing I can do.
I have to get to school.

I open the shed door and the light of the morning surprises me and hurts my eyes for a moment.

I have a shower and get dressed and make my way to school. Everything is strange. 'I only just came back from school,' I think. 'Is it really Tuesday?'
I get to school much earlier than I normally do. There aren't many people around, and I still have some time before school starts. And that is why I make an important decision.

I turn left towards the bus stop.

It's only 400 metres away from the school gates. I start running.
In the distance I can see two girls, pushing another girl. They are shouting at her. I run faster, as fast as I can. Soon, I am at the bus stop, and the two girls are standing there looking at a girl on the ground. They see me. And as soon as they see me, they run away.

It was Amy and Chloe. Just like it was in the shed. And it is Emma who is on the ground. I give her my hand and help her to get on her feet again.
'Are you okay?' I ask.
'Yes, …I'm, …Yes, …I'm, …. I'm, okay thank you,' says Emma.
Then she crosses the road and walks away.
I call her but it's like she can't hear me. She carries on walking and doesn't turn her head.
'Maybe she's going to catch a bus back home,' I think to myself. I watch Emma as she disappears into the distance. I look at the ground where Emma fell. And I see some keys and a mobile phone.

'They belong to Emma,' I say to myself. 'She lives near the jam factory. I'll take these things to her house after school.'

But what does after school mean now? Will Tuesday suddenly become Wednesday? What is this thing that I found in the garden? Why did I see the future like that?
These questions worry me, and I decide never to touch the pot again.
'It will stay in the shed for now and I'll decide where to take it later.' I think. . . . 'I'll take it to the forest and hide it so that no one can find it. I'll give it a new home. Maybe the pot is angry with me for taking it away from where I found it.'
This is the kind of thing I think as I walk into the school.

Chapter 3:

The Open Door

All week I think of nothing else. My head is full of questions.

'Why are Amy and Chloe so horrible to Emma?'
'What can I do to stop them from being horrible?'
'How can this pot do these things and tell me the future?'
'How did I jump in time like that?'
'What can I do with the pot?'

These were the questions on my mind all the time. By now I was sure that the pot was some kind of drum. The noise it made! It was so beautiful.

Beautiful and mysterious.

To be honest, I was very worried about what the drum might do next. And that is why I decided to never use it again.
The next day on Wednesday after school. I went to Emma's house. I gave the phone and the keys to her dad and then went home.
When I got home, I didn't go to the shed. It didn't feel right, and I wasn't ready.
What I didn't know was that the drum was ready for me. And it let me know.

At 10pm I get ready for bed. I have a shower, clean my teeth, and put on my pyjamas. And then I get into bed. But the moment I close my eyes I hear that sound again.

'Creak!!!'

It's louder than the last time. It doesn't last for very long. But I know that it's the drum and it wants to tell me something.
But what?
Every night when I go to bed, the sound of the drum gets louder and louder. And the sound lasts longer and longer.
On Thursday it lasts about ten minutes.
On Friday it's even louder and lasts about one hour.
On Saturday I have to cover my ears because it's so loud, and it just won't stop. Hours pass and I can still hear it.

'Creak Creak Creak Creak Creak Creak Creak Creak Creak Creak Creak Creak!!!'

On Sunday the sound never ends. I can't turn it off. It doesn't stop.
On that night, it's impossible to sleep and so I open my eyes. In the darkness I can see something. It's a door and it's right in front of me. On the front of the door, I can see a picture of the sun. It's the same picture that is on the drum.

It's just too much. I can't stand it anymore. I go outside into my garden, open the door of the shed, and turn the light on. The drum is there waiting for me. I take it out and start to play.

'Tap Tap Tap'

At first just a few taps.

'Tap Tap Tap Tap Tap Tap Tap!' Then some more taps.

Something starts happening. In front of me very slowly I see something. At first, I don't know what it is. But then I understand. It's a very old door. It's like a door that is thousands and thousands of years old. It's huge and tall and heavy.
Then I hear the sound again.

'Creak!!!'

The door opens.
At first, I just see light. I don't know why but I don't feel frightened. The light feels nice. It watches over me, and it's friendly.

When the door is completely open, I hear the sound of a woman. She's singing. The song is familiar, but distant so I can't understand what it is. It all happens in a microsecond and the music suddenly disappears.

Then through the light something else comes out. Not something I can hear but something I can see. I'm not sure what it is at first. But then I see some numbers.

The numbers are.

6 1 4 1 3 1 2

Is it a phone number? Then there are more numbers.

6 8 0 2 9 4 9

The numbers then disappear at the same time as the light. I jump as I hear the door shutting loudly.

'Bang!'

And then I don't remember anything else. I don't remember going back into the house. I don't remember going back to bed. All I know is that I wake up the next morning in my bedroom. Was it all a dream? It just seemed to be too real for that. Just too real.
One thing I did know for sure. I wasn't frightened. That light! It showed me that the drum is my friend, and it wants me to play it.

Chapter 4:

My Drum, My Friend

What happened that night changes me completely. I cannot just leave the drum in the shed and forget about it. I have to be nice to the drum. It's my friend and I can't just ignore it.
I still have the feeling that the light I saw that night is kind. 'The drum won't do anything bad to me. It helped Emma that day,' I think. 'And it wants to help me.'
And so, every day I play my drum. I play it with all of my heart. I love the sound it makes and after a while my hands seem to move by themselves as I tap all over it. I play it with love and with happiness. I play it like it is a part of me. Every day the sounds come from the garden shed. But my dad doesn't hear a thing. I make sure that he doesn't hear it or see it. He is always out when I play. I worry about him worrying. My dad and I, we look after each other like that. I try to protect him, and he tries to protect me. I have the feeling that dad hearing the drum is not a good idea.

Every day after school, I play the drum. And it thanks me in its own way and tells me something important. I see something that is going to happen in the future.
I become quite a good drummer. Maybe even good enough to play drums for Crispy Street.

When I make the decision to do what the drum wants and to play it, I feel better. The drum feels better too. On one afternoon I play the drum, I hear the door open, I see the light and then I find myself in my classroom. The classroom is empty, and my teacher is sitting at his desk, looking at some papers. I can see the clock on the wall. It's 9.50 am. I usually have my Maths lesson at ten.

The drum lets me get closer to what my teacher is looking at. Now I can see what he is seeing. I see the date on the paper. It's tomorrow! Then I see the words, Class 5b. That's my class. And then I see that it is a test.
'It's the test I have to do tomorrow!' I say to myself. Luckily, I'm very good at remembering numbers!

The next day I'm in the classroom. The clock strikes ten and the test begins. I finish really quickly. And while I wait for the others to finish, I silently thank my drum.
I get my first ever 'A' in Maths.

After many afternoons of playing the drum, an idea comes into my head. The drum always decides what it wants me to see. But what if I tell the drum what I want to see. If I ask nicely, will it tell me?

Chapter 5:

Asking

The next day I begin my little experiment.
'What do I want to see?' I ask myself. 'What do I want to know?' An idea comes to me, and I start drumming. I'm not sure what to say. How do you ask a drum to help you?

I decide that the best way to ask a drum to do something for you is to do the same thing that you do with a real-life person. I was nice and polite.

'Please can you tell me where Owen Banks will be tomorrow? Thank you.'

I keep playing, and then I hear the door, the light comes and then in its place I see Owen Banks, the drummer from Crispy Street sitting on a train. He looks at his mobile phone and I can see that it's 10.40 am on a Saturday morning.

And that is why I get on the train at Rayleigh station at 10.25 on a Saturday morning and make my way towards a certain carriage. I get to the carriage and see Owen Banks.

'Erm, Hi. I'm a fan. My name's Nathan. Can I have your autograph, please?'

'Oh yeah! Sure. But I haven't got a ...'

'I have one,' I say. Of course, I do. I know exactly what's going to happen. I give him a pen and a piece of paper. And that piece of paper is now on my bedroom wall. Owen Banks, the best drummer in the world.

It's strange but when I was there, in front of my hero, I could see that he was pleased to give a fan an autograph. But somehow, I couldn't just see that he was pleased. I could also feel it. I could feel his happiness and that made me feel happy all day. I couldn't stop smiling.

The next day I ask the drum something else.
'Please can you tell me where Emma is? Thank you'. I feel that the thank you part of my request is important.
Soon the door opens for me, and I see Emma at the lake near my school. I watch her throw a little stone into the water.

Plop!

She looks very sad. I see her sitting there, and the same thing happens to me again. The same thing that happened with Owen Banks. I don't only see her reaction I feel it too. This time the feeling is not a nice one. I can feel her pain. I know that she is crying inside. She is so sad. But what is she sad about? I'm not sure. I feel like her, and it hurts. The feeling of sadness stays with me all day.
Because of what happened with Owen Banks and Emma, I begin to understand that asking the drum what I want to see is a dangerous thing. It not only shows me things that are going to happen in the future. It also gets me to feel things. To feel how Owen and Emma feel.

This is why most of the time I play the drum because it wants me to play it. And I wait for the drum to tell me what it wants to tell me.
I play the drum and see my next-door neighbour's cat. It's nighttime. The cat is frightened and crying and is sitting

under a car in Oxford Street. I recognise the car. It's quite old. No one uses it and it is always parked there.

The next night I walk to the car. I call out to the cat. I have some biscuits for her and shake the box and say,
'Amber! Come here. Come with me. Good kitty. There you are!'
The cat comes into my arms, and I take it home. My neighbour is so happy.
'She was lost,' she said. 'I couldn't find her anywhere! Thank you, Nathan.'

I play the drum, and it helps me to do so many things, to make me happy and to make other people happy too.

Time passes by so quickly and soon it is my birthday. A birthday is always a special day for everyone. But my dad made it an extra special day for me because he bought me something I wanted so much. He bought me a bicycle.
I was the luckiest boy in the world. I had everything I wanted, didn't I?

Well, I didn't really have everything I wanted.

I didn't have the one thing I wanted most in the world.

I didn't have mum.

Chapter 6:

Not Just Any Sun

I go out on my new bicycle every day. It's great because I can connect it to my phone and see how many miles I have travelled. Then I can post it online.
On the Saturday after my birthday, I send a message to my friend, Anne.
'Do you want to come out for a bike ride?'
'Where to?' replies Anne.
'I don't know, somewhere out of town. Let's see how far we can go.'
'Great,' said Anne. 'Shall I invite Jack?'
'Sure,' I say.
I make some sandwiches and then cycle to the park to meet my friends.
It's 9 am when we set out and we decide to head to the southeast where the countryside is.

Soon we are out of town. It's nice to be out because it gives me a chance to think of other things and not just the drum. I think about Emma most of the time. Emma is interesting, different from the other girls. I want to know why she is so sad, and I want to find out more about her.
It's good to feel the wind against my arms and we ride for about two hours, passing different towns and travelling along the country lanes. Anne is always in the front, then Jack and then me. I like being at the back.

After about two hours, we arrive at a town called Paglesham. I have always liked that name. Paglesham! It sounds so cool. Three syllables. /Pa/gel/shem/. We decide to stop there and eat our sandwiches.

The sandwiches are good, but they make me thirsty.
'I didn't bring anything to drink,' I say to the others. 'You go on. I'll meet you outside Canewdon church, in an hour.'
My friends agree and I get off my bike and walk through the town centre, so that I can find a place to get a quick drink. There aren't many shops because it's a very small town. But as I walk, I see something and stop. There is something that catches my eye on my left.
It's an old wooden door. And on the door, there is a drawing of the sun.
But it isn't just any sun.
It's just like the drawing on the drum.
Identical!
I stop for a little while to look at the drawing. How is this possible? Where does it come from? It's exactly the same so, what does this mean? All of these questions start running through my head.
I look at my phone to see what the time is. It's only 11 am. I have some time to see what's inside. Canewdon is only about forty-five minutes away.
I knock on the door. I just can't stop myself from doing it. I don't think about who might be behind the door.

'Knock Knock!'

No answer. I stand there a little while longer, scratching my head. What should I do now?
And then without thinking about it, I start to open the door. What am I doing? This just isn't me. I don't do this kind of thing. I push harder and open the door.

'Creak!!!'

It was the same sound! The sound that the drum makes when it wants me to play it.
The door is completely open now, and I look inside. What I see is incredible and I will remember it for the rest of my life. I will never forget it. Never!

Chapter 7:

Chimaobi

It's quite dark so I can't see many details at first. But I do know immediately that the room I am in doesn't belong in Paglesham. And it doesn't belong to this century. It looks like a house in another place far away from England, far away from Europe, in another time.
To my left there is a fireplace and in front of the fire there is a woman sitting on a chair. She moves the chair backwards and forwards, backwards and forwards.
I just stand there with my mouth open. I don't know what to do or what to say. My feet can't move. I can't go out of the room and close the door. Something stops me. I remain there for what feels like forever.

And then the woman turns towards me and smiles.
The smile is friendly.

'Finally. You're here,' says the woman.
'I'm sorry, but do, do I know you?' I ask. And as I say these words, I try to smile to hide my confusion.
The woman notices that I am not sure of myself and says, 'Don't worry. I'm your friend. You don't know me. But I know you.'

I stand there and don't speak for a while. I can't. Here I am in the middle of this town that I don't know very well and this woman in this strange room is talking to me calmly. She knows me and isn't surprised to see me.

She knew I was going to come knocking on her door.

'My name is Chimaobi,' she says.
'Pleased to meet you Chim, Chimaobi,' I say.
I don't pronounce her name well and so she gently corrects me by repeating it. I silently put the words into syllables.
'Chim/a/o/bi'
'Chim a o bi,' I repeat. 'It's nice to meet you. This house looks different from the other houses around here,' I say.
'Oh, it won't be here long,' says Chimaobi. 'I just came here to speak to you.'
'Sorry did you say it won't be here long? Do you mean that the house won't be here long? Or you? I'm confused. And you want to speak to me? You came here only to speak to me. But why? Why do you want to speak to me? I don't know you. You must think I'm somebody else. I'm, I'm sorry, I'll go, I'll ...'

'Nathan!' says Chimaobi.

That stops me from moving away.
'How do you know my name?' I ask. 'How is that possible?'
'We both have the same friend. You met not long ago.' says Chimaobi.
'I haven't met anyone new, recently,' I reply.
Chimaobi is still smiling. And as she smiles, her fingers tap on the side of the chair.
As soon as I see this, I know why she is here. She's talking about the drum.
'The drum? You want the drum,' I ask.
The old lady stops smiling and looks straight at me. 'The Udu drum,' she says. 'The drum is tired. The drum wants to rest. The drum needs peace.'
'I understand,' I say.
But I don't really understand. Nothing makes sense.

'I know what is happening inside your head,' says the woman. 'I know what you're thinking. And I can tell you not to worry. You will understand soon. I promise.'
And then she smiles at me again. It's the sweetest smile I have ever seen. Then I hear some soft music in the background. The woman is singing and the music seems familiar and safe and warm. The smile and the music make me feel calm, even at a moment like this when I don't know what to do and what to say and how to think. I don't know if it is best to run away or to sit down and cry. Even at a moment like this, I really want to close my eyes.
And so, I close them just for a second. Just to rest them.

And then I hear a voice. A gentle voice. It's a voice that I know.

'Kulie N'ura'.

When I open my eyes, Chimaobi isn't there anymore. The house isn't there either. I am standing in the middle of the street with my phone in my hand and my bike against the wall.
'What's happening to me?' I say to myself. 'Was I sleeping? Was I dreaming?'
And then I shout.
'I just wanted to go out for a normal bike ride with my friends.'
'Can't I have a normal life?'
No one is listening. This was Paglesham on a Saturday morning. There was no one around to hear me or answer my desperate question.

I text Jack and Anne to tell them I have to get back home and then ride to my town and my house as fast as I can.

Chapter 8:

A Familiar Face

As I ride home, I think of what Chimaobi has said. Now I know that the drum has a name.

The Udu drum.

I also know that it's time to speak to dad. Maybe he knows something that will help me. I can't hide the drum from him anymore.

Everything is so strange but somehow, I know that Chimaobi is a friend. I am not afraid. It's time to share my story with dad.

Dad doesn't have many friends. Not since mum died. When mum died all the joy in his life seemed to leave him. He doesn't smile much. But when he smiles it is a precious moment. I love to see him smile. The only thing that makes him happy is when we talk about the past. He lives in a present that doesn't belong to him. I don't think he'll ever be happy again. Mum was everything to him and when she went the lights went out for dad too.

I only know one thing that always puts a smile on his face. It never fails. The photos!

As soon as I get home, I have a quick shower and change into some comfortable clothes. Then I go into the living room. Dad is there, sitting in his armchair.

'Hi Nathan,' says dad. 'Did you have a good day?'

'It was ..., well it was different,' I say.
'Did you go out on your bike?'
'Yes, dad. I went out with Anne and Jack. In fact, I'm quite tired now and think I'm going to stay in tonight. Why don't we get some pizza, relax and we can look at some of the old photos together?'
'Okay,' says dad. 'I'll go and get them.'
'Fantastic!' I say. 'I'll order the pizza.'

After eating, we sit at the dinner table and pick up the first photo album. Dad turns the pages slowly and we comment on each photo.
There is a picture of mum and dad standing in front of a theatre in London. I remember that day! We had tickets to see the musical 'Mamma Mia' and we were so excited.
Then there is another photo of mum in front of a castle, another of dad trying to put up a tent, me dancing at Uncle Brian's third wedding, mum holding cousin Charlotte when she was a tiny baby. All photos of a time when there were three of us. We were a team, mum, dad and I.

Mum was either in the photo or she was the one who pointed the camera. She was everywhere.

There were photos of parties, weddings and family celebrations. There were lots of smiling faces of people on holiday. Uncles and aunties, cousins and babies. We looked at ourselves in front of the Eiffel Tower, inside the Colosseum, on the top of a mountain in the Alps and on a boat on the river Thames.
We remembered together. The first photos were the oldest. Dad liked to look through them in order. He liked it this way because then he could control things. Real life was full of surprises and here, in this place, he didn't want any

surprises. He wanted to know exactly where each photo was.
He turned the pages slowly, looking from left to right, reliving every moment, and remembering.
He always slowed down when he got near to that date. August 2013.

The pages turned slowly, so slowly.

After that date there were no more photos of mum. He always wanted to stop before that date, so that we didn't have to think of the terrible moment when mum's favourite chair in the living room was empty, forever, to that moment when there were two of us and not three.
Seeing the photos again made us laugh and cry. It always did. Both dad and I smiled and cried, sometimes at the same time. It was beautiful and it was terrible. Soft sweet music, and silent screams of lonely sadness for things that will never return.

Oh mum! Oh mum! How much I miss you! How much I want to tell you about the drum. How much I miss your smile and your voice. I want you to be proud of me. I hope you are still there, proud of who I am, and who I will become.

Dad turned the pages of the photo album Slower and slower as the years went past. 2010, 2011, 2012, getting closer and closer to that date when time seemed to stop forever.

'Wait' I shout suddenly.
'Stop dad! Stop there! This photo! Who? Sorry! But who is that woman next to mum? Who is she?' I ask.

I point to a woman in the photo. She has her arm around mum's shoulder. She is smiling as she looks at the camera. I know that smile. I know it so well.

'Oh! That's Chimaobi,' says dad. 'A friend of your mum.'

I can't say anything to dad but inside my mind is racing. My heart is beating faster than my bicycle. Chimaobi the woman I saw in Paglesham is the woman in that photo. What does this mean?
I didn't get an answer to this question. Instead of getting answers I just had more and more questions and they kept coming into my mind one after the other. But they didn't come to me in an orderly way, one by one like dad's photos. All of the questions arrived at the same time. Luckily dad was concentrating so much on the photos that he didn't notice my confusion.

Chimaobi was mum's friend. I let this thought stay in my head for a few seconds, and then I made a decision. It was time to tell dad everything.
'Dad' I say. 'There is something I have to tell you.'

Dad listens to what I have to say. I tell him everything from that first night when I heard the sound in the garden to the bike ride to Paglesham. There is no expression on his face as he listens. He doesn't say anything and when I get to the part where I speak about Chimaobi, he stands up and says, 'Nathan, I'm tired. And you are too. It's hard for both of us, I know. We'll talk some more tomorrow.'

And with those words he walks out of the room and goes to bed. Dad was wrong. I wasn't tired.
I was ready to do some drumming.

OUR FAMILY

Chapter 9:

A Little Research

By now I know that there is a connection between my mum, Chimaobi and the drum.
I think about what Chimaobi said to me about the drum in Paglesham, and I want to find out more. Thanks to her now I know what I'm looking for.
I switch on my phone and say the key words.

'Udu'

'Drum'

'Nigeria.'

And soon I find something of interest.

> *"The Udu drum is a kind of pot that belongs to the culture of the Igbo people in Southeast Nigeria."*
>
> *"Originally Igbo women did not use it as a drum but as a way of carrying water from the river. They also used it in the kitchen to cook."*
>
> *"While getting the water, the Igbo women made music by singing and tapping on the pot."*
>
> *"The body of the Udu drum has one or more holes which you can cover or uncover to make different sounds."*
>
> *"There are some modern-day versions of the Udu Drum. For example, 'Planet Drum' made in the mountains of South Tyrol in Italy"*

As I read, certain words hit me.

Igbo People Nigeria

Carry water.

Sing and tap on the pot.

One or more holes.

I look for some more information about Igbo people. They come from Southeast Nigeria. I know that already. So, I start to look for important towns and cities in the area.
Soon I find the city of Onitsha which is on the river Niger. I remember mum talking about this river! Then I google for more information. As soon as the next page loads, I see some numbers on the page that aren't new to me.

6.141312

6.802949

Once again, my good memory for numbers helps me. The numbers are latitude and longitude of the city of Onitsha in Southeast Nigeria.

They were the numbers that the drum showed to me on that night! The night when the drum opened the door for the first time. Now I knew the precise location of the drum. I knew where it belonged.

So, this is what it was. It was an Udu drum. A kind of drum that was a part of my mum's culture. Maybe she had one in her house when she was young. Maybe her grandmother used it. My great grandmother.

I was quite young when mum died that I never really had a chance to know much about her life before me, and before she moved to the UK. But I am a part of that life. I come from her. I am connected to the drum, just like her. The drum belongs to me too.
I sit there thinking of all these things and what they mean. And then my mind goes back to Paglesham. I think of Chimaobi's smile and the music I heard that day. Why did that music make me feel sleepy? Why was it so warm and familiar?

Suddenly I know why. It was THE song. The song that I was so frightened of singing. It was the song that mum sang to me when I was a little boy.

Suddenly everything starts to make sense. Mum is trying to tell me something.

She is asking me to wake up.

And now I know what I have to do.

Chapter 10:

The Midnight Sky

I go into the shed and look at the drum. It's getting dark.
'I'm going to play you now,' I say to the drum. 'But this time it's going to be different. This time it won't be just you and me.'

I sit down and get ready.
But before I start, I hear a noise.

'Knock! Knock!'

I know who it is. I know because after doing my research, I asked the drum a question, and it gave me the answer.

I know who is behind that door and I know how that person feels. He feels like me. I open the door.
It's dad.
'Let's see the drum,' he says as he enters the shed.
I show him the drum. And he picks it up.
'So, this is the pot, sorry, the drum that helps you to see all these things,' he says. 'I'm sorry Nathan. I try to understand. But it's difficult.'
'I'll help you to understand,' I say. 'Don't worry dad. Listen to me carefully.'
'In ten seconds, you'll hear the beginning of a really big storm.'
I start the countdown. 10, 9, 8, 7, 6, 5, 4, 3, 2,

1.

We see an enormous flash of light outside the shed window, and then we hear a big noise.

'Kerasssshhhhhhhhhhhhhh!!!'

Thunder!

I look at dad's face. It seems different. His face looks more alive. It has more colour in it than usual. He's beginning to understand.

'Nathan,' he says excitedly, 'this means that the drum is real. That what you are saying is true. And it means that your mum ... is here.' he says, moving his arms around the shed almost like he's trying to touch her. His face by now is shining like the sun on the drum.
'Yes, dad. It's real. And mum has come to tell us something.'
'What?' asks dad. 'What is it?'

'Kulie N'ura', I say.

Dad looks at me, still trying to understand.

'It's time to wake up, dad. Mum is saying that we have to think of the future now. No more living in the past. We have to let her go. She loves us. But she wants to go home. It's time to live our lives!'
I take the drum from dad and walk out of the shed. Dad follows me. It's raining hard but we don't care.
'We can let her go now, dad,' I shout. 'She's okay. We can let her go home. She wants us to be happy. She wants us to sing her song and make our own future.' Dad stands there with his mouth open. He cannot believe it. He looks

up at the sky, and then he smiles. I hold the drum. I don't care about the rain. And, I start to tap and sing.
I sing mum's song. I'm not afraid of singing it anymore. I remember all the words; every single word comes to me as I drum. My hands move with my voice. The vibration of my voice and of the drum seem to belong to each other. The rain goes on and on around us. The drum is heavy because the rain is filling it up. But I keep singing and drumming, singing and drumming. I see dad's face through the rain. He's still smiling as he stands there, watching and listening and looking up at the sky.
I keep singing and playing, singing and playing. The words, the beat of the drum and the rain seem to make a symphony and it goes on and on and on until dad says,

'Nathan!'
'What dad?'
'The drum. It's not here anymore!'

I look at my hands and I see that they are empty. I see that there is no drum. The rain stops. I look at dad and he looks at me. He puts his arms around me, and we hug each other.

And we make our own rain as we cry and cry and cry under the midnight sky.

Six months later . . .

So now you know my story.

I will never forget that night in the garden. Things changed for dad and for me after that.

The beat of the drum is the beat of life. We must go on. We cannot stop.

Mum is happy now and she wants us to be happy too. She wants us to do new things so that we can take photos of new moments and look forward not back. She wants us to make our own future.

That is the lesson of the drum.

I spoke to Emma last week. We had a really nice conversation. She is very special. I don't know what will happen between us. But I like not knowing the future. It's better that way.

Whatever happens I know that I will always hear the gentle voice of my mother saying

'Kulie N'ura'.

As I start a new day.

The Origin of the Planet Drum

This is my sound!

In chapter 9 of the story, Nathan finds out that the drum was originally a container that women used to bring back water from the river for their families. They used the pot to make music while they were there.
So, how did a drum that started its life on the banks of a river in Nigeria became the inspiration for Barbara, who lives in the mountains of South Tyrol in Italy?
It all began when Barbara went to a percussion workshop, and she heard a man playing the drum. She loved the sound the drum made. It was an Udu drum. This is my sound, she said.

What is Barbara's drum like?

After doing many experiments in her studio and trying a number of different techniques she finally created her own version of the drum. Barbara's drum is round and has a diameter of about 33 centimetres. It has two sound holes of different sizes, and these holes help the drummer to make its unique sound. You can find examples of her work on her website.

It takes about 3 weeks to make each drum and Barbara enjoys making them so much that while she works, she thinks about what the next planet drum will look like. Every drum is different and has its own sound.

How do you play the drum?
The drummer taps different parts of the drum and covers the holes at different times with their hands and this makes it possible to make a lot of different sounds.

Top left: Playing together
Bottom Left: Display of Planet Drums

Right: Barbara at MART (Museo di arte moderna e contemporanea di Trento e Rovereto)

Planet Drums: http://www.planet-drum.it

About the Illustrators

Bethany Lacey-Freeman

Hi! Thank you for reading *The Drum*! I hope you have enjoyed this latest addition to the *Egghead* universe. It was so much fun gathering research and designing characters for this story. I am thankful for Craig's assistance with the backgrounds and colour palettes as well as his willingness to watch plenty of Nollywood media with me!

Working alongside Michael and Craig is always fun and it's great that we get to work together to bring you all more stories.

I always enjoy illustrating Nathan, Emma and their friends and I'm looking forward to Michael bringing them back for more adventures in the future!

You can find my work on Instagram and Facebook!

Instagram: bethlf_illustrates

Facebook: Bethany Lacey-Freeman Illustration

About the Illustrators

Craig Bulloch

Hello! I hope you've enjoyed reading this story, as much as I have working on the illustrations. Our aim is to bring the people and places in the story alive! In Michael's last book, *Egghead the Movie,* I worked alongside fellow Illustrator, Bethany Lacey-Freeman, to create great characters that represented Michael's vision of the characters he was writing about, and it was great that some of them appeared also in this book.

During the time working on the *Egghead the Movie* project I discovered a new passion for designing and illustrating backgrounds, and so for this project I concentrated mostly on creating the backgrounds for each illustration. This worked well because Bethany is an amazing character artist! Her talent for creating expressions and different poses for her characters is brilliant.

You can find my work on Instagram and Facebook!

Instagram: ryukicomics
Facebook: Ryuki Comics

About the Author

Michael Lacey Freeman

Hello! My name is Michael Lacey Freeman, and I am the writer of this story. I come from a town called Rochford, near London in the UK but I live and work in Italy now.
I love reading stories and I am lucky that I have the opportunity to actually write stories too. I share my stories with people all over the world and have recently been to Indonesia, Vietnam and Mongolia to spread the message that words are powerful. I have told my stories to many people online too.
I also love music and make songs with my band, *The Eggheads*. We make songs for the stories I write and the song for this story is called, *I'm Afraid*. You can visit our Youtube channel, *Lorenzo Paoloni & Michael Lacey Freeman* if you want to hear more of our songs.

The Stories
Perhaps my most popular story is *Egghead*. It is a story about a little boy who is bullied at school. It is a true story. I should know that it is true because the little boy in the story was me. Recently I have written a sequel to this story, called *Egghead the Movie*. I have written other stories like *Dot to Dot*, All *the Colours of Sam, Boloroo's Big Question,* and of course, *The Drum*. Now I am writing another story called, *The Overnight Success*.

The Drum
If you have already read, Egghead the Movie you may realise that some of the characters from that story are in this story too. I really enjoyed writing The Drum. I understand Nathan because I love sounds too. And I also love music.

Losing Someone
We all know how difficult it is when we have to say goodbye to someone. It might not even be a person. It might be a pet or even a place. Sometimes we only really understand how important someone, or something is when we don't have it anymore. That is why it is important to be grateful for what we have right now, in this moment. And to be positive about the future. Nathan's mother taught him a lot of things and Nathan learnt to be grateful for that too. The cultural connection he has with Nigeria, his love of music, a love for life in general, and his mother left him an important message.

'Kulie N'ura'

The Theme Song of The Drum

'I'm Afraid'

(Paoloni/Lacey Freeman)

Last night I had another dream
And it was surrounding me
It was clear
It was clear

And every time and every day
In every way I know I'll pay
I'm afraid, I'm afraid

And every time you say my name
Well, I go on I feel no shame
It's too late
It's too late

Last night I had another dream
And it was surrounding me
It was near
It was fear

And every night I will be there
And my fears live everywhere
It was clear
It was near

And every time and every day
In every way I know I'll pay
I'm afraid, I'm afraid

And every time you say my name
Well, I go on I feel no shame
It's too late
It's too late

And every time and every day
In every way I know I'll pay
I'm afraid, I'm afraid

Visit Lorenzo and Michael on their youtube channel:
Lorenzo Paoloni & Michael Lacey Freeman
https://www.youtube.com/user/hev477b

Where you will find the theme song to **The Drum** - 'I'm Afraid'

Other songs include:

- **Egghead the Movie** - 'Got Something to Tell You' plus 'Beside You'

- **Boloroo's BIG Question** - 'Butterfly'

- **Egghead** - 'Crying'

- 'Freeworld'

- 'Identity - All of My Fires'

- 'I'm Not There'

And many more songs, interviews and videos.

Exercises – Test Your Knowledge

Chapter 1: The Sound of Music

Reading Comprehension

1. Decide if the sentences are true (T) or false (F).

		T/F
a)	Nathan plays in a band called Crispy Street.	___
b)	Nathan's mum was from Nigeria.	___
c)	Kulie N'ura means 'Go to sleep.'	___
d)	Nathan sees a strange object in the garden.	___
e)	Nathan was in the garden for five minutes.	___
f)	The weather is very calm.	___

Grammar

2. Complete the sentences from chapter 1 by using the words below.

always   never   normally   often   sometimes

a) Nathan _____ listens to the music of his favourite band.
b) Nathan's mum _____ sang the same song to him.
c) Nathan has a memory of his mother that will _____ go away.
d) _____, Nathan wakes up to his mother's voice even now.
e) When Nathan listens to music _____ he doesn't hear anything else.

3. Read this extract from chapter 1 and decide if you need the article, 'the' or not.

I love *(a) the* sound of the drums. I like to drum on *(b) the* my desk at school, but I can't do it too much because *(c) the* teacher stops me. I drum on anything, on *(d) the* my legs when I'm sitting down, on *(e) the* dining table at home, on *(f) the* walls of my bedroom. Dad says that one day he'll buy me a set of *(g) the* real drums, but I think he's worried about *(h) the* noise I will make.

Vocabulary

4. Unjumble the words from chapter 1.

   a) GNOS _____   e) MROST _____
   b) TASNICUR _____ f) TERSAOT _____
   c) RUMSD. _____   g) DSHE _____
   d) CHROT _____   h) TOP _____

In Your Own Words

5. Can you remember what sounds Nathan likes?

6. What sounds do you like the most?

7. What songs are special to you?

8. What songs make you think of other people who are special in your life?

9. What songs make you feel happy or sad?

10. Make a playlist of songs that are your own personal soundtrack to this story.

Chapter 2: Bus Stop Hero

Reading

1. Match the questions to the answers.

   a) What is Abacha?
   b) Why does Nathan leave the drum over the weekend?
   c) Who are Jack and Anne?
   d) Who is Emma?
   e) What does Nathan see on the drum when he cleans it?
   f) What happens when Nathan starts tapping on the drum?

   1) They are Nathan's friends.
   2) Because he doesn't want any mystery.
   3) He sees his school.
   4) She is the girl that Nathan likes.
   5) It's food from Nigeria.
   6) There is a picture of the sun.

Grammar

2. Complete the questions from chapter 2 with the question words below. Then check chapter two to see if your answers are correct.

   How   What   Where   Who   Why

1 _____? Mason Adderley?
2 _____ did it come from?
3 _____ is this possible.
4 _____ happened to the night-time?
5 _____ did I see the future like that?

Vocabulary

3. Write the opposite of these words and find them in chapter 2.

   a) Happy   _____   e) Ordinary _____
   b) Hot   _____   f) Bored   _____
   c) Early   _____   g) Short   _____
   d) Right   _____   h) Clean   _____

In Your Own Words

4. Do you like the title of this chapter? Think of an alternative title.

5. Think of a hobby that you have where time passes very quickly because you enjoy it so much. Does time fly for you when you do this activity.

6. Do you remember the name of the dish that Nathan's dad makes. Look up the recipe on the Internet. Would you like to eat it.

7. What dish is special from your country? Write a description of it for a guest from another country.

8. What things can you do if you know someone who is being bullied?

Chapter 3: The Open Door

Reading

1. Choose the correct word for each sentence.

> *door   drum   light   noise   numbers   song   sun*

    a) Nathan was worried about what the _____ might do next.
    b) The _____ of the drum gets louder and louder every night.
    c) On the front of the door there is a picture of the _____.
    d) Nathan sees an old _____ and then he sees a _____ which feels nice.
    e) Nathan hears a woman who sings a _____.
    f) After hearing the singing Nathan sees some _____.

Grammar

2. Unjumble the questions.

    a) horrible to Emma/Amy and Chloe/why are?
    b) to stop them/what can I do/from being so horrible?
    c) and tell me the future/do these things/how can the drum?
    d) like that/jump in time/how did I?
    e) can I do/what/with the pot?

In Your Own Words

3. Why is Nathan not frightened of the drum?

Chapter 4: My Drum, My Friend

Reading

1. Answer the questions in no more than four words.

   a) Where does Nathan keep the drum? _____
   b) Who doesn't know that Nathan plays the drum? _____
   c) At what time of day does Nathan play the drum? _____
   d) What does the drum take Nathan to see at his school?_____
   e) Why does Nathan do well in the Maths test? _____

Grammar

2. Choose the right option to complete this paragraph from chapter 4. Then check the chapter again to see if your answers are correct.

Every day the sounds *(1) come/comes* from the garden shed. But my dad *(2) don't/doesn't* hear a thing. I make sure that he doesn't hear it *(3) but/or* see it. He *(4) is always/always is* out when I play. I worry about him worrying. My dad and I, we look after each other *(5) as/like* that. I try to protect him, and he tries to protect me. I *(6) have/has* the feeling that dad hearing the drum is not a good idea.

In Your Own Words

3. Nathan is good at remembering numbers. Name three things that you are good at doing.

4. What subjects do you like best at school?

Chapter 5: Asking

Reading

1. Put the events in chapter five in the right order. Nathan

		Order
a)	gets on a train.	___
b)	celebrates his birthday!	___
c)	asks for Owen Banks' autograph.	___
d)	asks the drum where Owen Banks is.	___
e)	asks the drum where Emma is.	___
f)	saves the neighbour's cat.	___
g)	sees Emma by the lake.	___

Grammar

2. Complete the extract from chapter 5 with one word for each gap. Then check to see if your answer is correct.

It's strange (1) _____ when I was there, in front of my hero, I could see (2) _____ he was pleased to give a fan (3) _____ autograph. But somehow, I couldn't (4) _____ see that he was pleased. I could also feel it. I could feel (5) _____ happiness and that made me feel happy (6) _____ day. I couldn't stop smiling.

3. There are six extra words in this extract from chapter 5. Can you find them and take them out?

Soon the door opens for me, and I do see Emma at the lake near my school. I watch her throw a little stone into the water.

Plop!

She looks as very sad. I see her sitting there, and the same thing happens to me again. The same thing that happened with Owen Banks. I don't only see her reaction and I feel it too. This what time the feeling is not a nice one. I can feel her pain. I know that she is crying inside her. She is so sad. But what is she sad about? I'm not sure. I feel like her, and it hurts. The feeling of sadness is stays with me all day.

Vocabulary

4. Take a word or words from column A and match it to a word or words from column B to make an expression from chapter 5.

Column A	Column B
a) bedroom	1 person
b) night	2 of paper
c) real-life	3 street
d) mobile	4 wall
e) a piece	5 phone
f) next door neighbour's	6 time
g) Oxford	7 cat

Match number and letter in the right order.

__ & __ ; __ & __ ; __ & __ ; __ & __ ; __ & __ ; __ & __ ; __ & __ ;

In Your Own Words

5. What autograph of a famous person would you like to have?

6. Why do you think that some famous people do not like to give autographs?

7. Do you remember the character of Emma from another story? What story is it?

8. Imagine that you can find out about something that happens in the future. What would you like to know?

9. Why does Nathan decide that it's not a good idea to keep asking the drum questions about the future?

Chapter 6: Not Just Any Sun

Reading

1. Which sentences are true (T) and which are false (F)? Correct the false sentences to make them true.

		T/F
a)	Nathan, Jack and Anne go on the bike ride together.	___
b)	Nathan rides his bike behind Jack and Anne.	___
c)	Nathan likes the town of Paglesham because it has nice sandwiches.	___
d)	Nathan stops at the door because he hears a noise.	___
e)	Someone opens the door for Nathan.	___
f)	When the door opens, Nathan hears a sound that is very familiar.	___

Grammar

2. Put the conversation between Nathan and Anne in the right order.

		Order
a)	'I don't know, somewhere out of town. Let's see how far we can go.'	___
b)	'Where to? replies Anne.	___
c)	'Sure,' I say.	___
d)	'Do you want to come out for a bike ride?'	___
e)	'Great,' said Anne. 'Shall I invite Jack?'	___

3. Read this extract from chapter 6 and put the verbs below in the right place. Then check the chapter to see if your answers are correct.

be   do   push   stand   start   stop

I knock on the door. I just can't (1) _____ myself from doing it. I don't think about who might (2) _____ behind the door.

'Knock Knock!'

No answer. I (3) _____ there a little while longer, scratching my head. What should I (4) _____ now?
And then without thinking about it, I (5) _____ to open the door. What am I doing? This just isn't me. I don't do this kind of thing. I (6) _____ harder and open the door.

In Your Own Words

4. Nathan likes the sound the word 'Paglesham' makes. What words in English do you like the sound of? Break the word up into syllables and then tell the person next to you about your favourite word.

5. What are your favourite words in your own language?

6. Look back at the first six chapters and list the sounds that Nathan mentions in his story. How would you write these sounds in your language?

7. Do you like going on bike rides in your area? What places do you like to visit?

8. Write an email to a friend from another country. Describe a place that you really like in your area and tell your friend why you think they should visit this place.

Chapter 7: Chimaobi

Reading

1. Choose the correct answer, A, B, or C
1A. Nathan doesn't leave the strange house immediately because he
   a) can't move.
   b) is fascinated.
   c) likes the room.

1B. Nathan is surprised that the woman in the strange room
   a) lives in Nigeria.
   b) stays in her chair.
   c) is waiting for him.

1C. Nathan knows that the drum is also Chimaobi's friend because
   a) she knows Nathan's name.
   b) they have similar friends.
   c) of the way she moves her fingers.

1D. Chimaobi doesn't frighten Nathan because
   a) he feels sleepy.
   b) she has a sweet smile.
   c) she is inside his head.

1E. Nobody answers Nathan when he shouts 'Can I have a normal life?' because
   a) he is in a dream.
   b) nobody is nearby.
   c) people are sleeping.

Vocabulary

2. Complete the table below.

Noun	Verb	Adjective	Adverb
	to confuse	confusing	confusedly
calm	to be calm		
	to surprise		surprisingly
tiredness		tiring	tiredly
	to be peaceful		
normality	to be normal	normal	

In Your Own Words

3. What towns and places in your area are really quiet and peaceful in the mornings?

4. Do you think that all the people of Paglesham could see the house or only Nathan?

5. What is strange about the picture on page 42?

6. What do you think it means?

7. Think of an alternative title for this chapter.

Chapter 8: A Familiar Face

Reading

1. Why is Nathan's dad looking through the photo album so slowly?

   a) Because he likes looking at each photo in detail.
   b) Because he cannot remember some of the photos.
   c) Because he doesn't want to look at the most recent photos.

Writing

2. Write one sentence that explains your answer to question 1.

_____

Grammar

3. Choose the right word and then check the extract in chapter 8 to see if your answers are correct.

Dad doesn't have *(1) lot of/many/much* friends. Not since mum died. When mum died all the joy in his life seemed to *(2) leave/leaving/left* him. He doesn't smile much. But when he smiles it is a precious moment. I love *(3) to see/to seen/to seeing* him smile. The only thing *(4) who/when/that* makes him happy is when we talk *(5) around/about/above* the past. He lives in a present that doesn't belong to him. I don't think he'll ever be happy again. Mum was *(6) everything/everyone/everybody* to him and when she went the lights went out for dad too.

Vocabulary

4. Match a word from column A to a word from column B to make an expression from chapter 8.

Column A	Column B
a) Living	1 celebrations
b) photo	2 ride
c) family	3 table
d) bike	4 room
e) dinner	5 drum
f) Udu	6 album

Match number and letter in the right order.

__ & __ ; __ & __ ; __ & __ ; __ & __ ; __ & __ ; __ & __ ;

5. Look at this extract from chapter 8 and complete it with the correct preposition.

There were photos (1) _____ parties, weddings and family celebrations. There were lots of smiling faces of people (2) _____ holiday. Uncles and aunties, cousins and babies. We looked (3) _____ ourselves (4) _____ front of the Eiffel Tower, inside the Colosseum, on the top of a mountain and (5) _____ a boat on a river.

In Your Own Words

6. What photos do you have that you would like to keep forever? Why are they so important?

Chapter 9: A Little Research

Reading

1. Correct the information about the Udu drum. There are six mistakes.

"The Udo drum is a kind of pot that belongs to the culture of the Igbo People in Southeast Kenya."
"Originally the Igbo women used it as a drum and as a way of carrying water from the river. They never used it in the kitchen to cook."
"While getting the water, the Igbo women made food by singing and tapping on the pot."
"The body of the Udu drum has two or more holes which you can cover or uncover to make different sounds."

Grammar

2. Choose the right word from this extract.

I was (a) quite/too young when mum died (b) which/that I never really had a chance to know much (c) in/about her life before me, and before she moved to the UK. (d) But/Because I am a part of that life. I come from her. I am connected (e) at/to the drum, just like her. (f) A/The drum belongs to me too.

In Your Own Words

3. What objects do you have that connect you to members of your family or to your culture?

4. 'Now I know what I have to do.' What do you think Nathan does after saying this?

Chapter 10: Under the Midnight Sky

Grammar

1. Read the extract from chapter 10 and choose the right option. Then read the chapter again to see if your answers are correct.

I keep singing and playing, singing and playing. The words, the beat (1) _____ the drum and the rain seem to make a symphony and it goes on and on and on (2) _____ dad says,

'Nathan!'
'What dad?'
'The drum. It's not there anymore!'

I look at (3) _____ hands and I see that they are empty. I see that there is no drum. The rain stops. I look at dad and he looks at me. He puts his arms (4) _____ me, and we hug (5) _____ other.

And we (6) _____ our own rain as we cry and cry and cry under the midnight sky.

Vocabulary

2. Complete the table with words you have seen in the story. Then add other words you know that belong to the same category.

The weather	Rain,
Rooms	Kitchen,
Types of Music	Rock,
Emotions	Sad,

Talking Points

How does Nathan know who is knocking at the door?

How does Nathan know exactly when a storm is about to start?

What is the message that Nathan's mum has for her son and her husband?

Why are Nathan and his dad hugging each other at the end of the story.

In Your Own Words

1. Did you enjoy the story?

2. What was your favourite chapter?

3. Think of another title for the story?

4. Listen to the theme tune of the story, 'I'm Afraid'. Do you think the song captures the spirit of the story?

5. Do you think that there will be romance between Nathan and Emma?

6. What is your favourite illustration in the story?

Writing

Write a review of the story. Post it on the Internet or show your class.

NOTE:

Additional resources available by emailing
michaellaceyfreeman@gmail.com
(Please include your school's name)

More Stories Published by Michael Lacey Freeman . . . .

Emma is bullied every day. The only time she's happy is when she draws. When she draws a picture, it feels like she can create a new world from nothing. And right now, she needs a new world because the world she lives in isn't a happy one. But there is someone who can help her.

Boloroo is a curious girl who always asks questions. She needs to know things like why the sky is blue, what stars are made of, and where babies come from. When she gets an answer to one question there is always another one she needs to ask. But there is one question that nobody can answer. It is her big question. Can you answer it?

Coming later this year . . . .

The Overnight Success - Marco doesn't like himself very much. His life is boring and he doesn't have any friends. He doesn't go out because nobody wants to spend time with him. All of this changes for Marco one winter morning when he wakes up to find that he is the most popular boy in the school. What happened and why? Marco decides to find out.

Boloroo: The Next Adventure – *What are Boloroo's questions when she goes on a new adventure? Read the second part of the Boloroo story. Coming soon!*

For more information check out Michael's website:
www.michaellaceyfreeman.com

www.ingramcontent.com/pod-product-compliance
Lightning Source LLC
Chambersburg PA
CBHW072130070526
44585CB00016B/1612